BESIDE THE SEASIDE

SEASIDE HOLIDAYS
THEN AND NOW

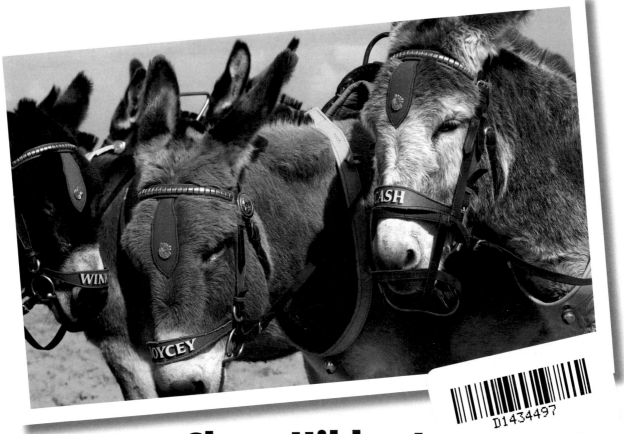

Clare Hibbert

W

Franklin Watts
Published in Great Britain in 2017
by The Watts Publishing Group

Planning and production by Discovery Books Limited
Managing editor: Paul Humphrey
Editor and picture researcher: Clare Hibbert
Design: sprout.uk.com

ISBN 978 1 4451 3758 2

Dewey classification number: 394.2'69'146

Printed in China

Franklin Watts
An imprint of Hachette Children's Group
Part of The Watts Publishing Group
Carmelite House
50 Victoria Embankment
London EC4Y 0DZ

An Hachette UK Company
www.hachette.co.uk
www.franklinwatts.co.uk

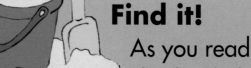

Find it!

As you read this book, look out for the hidden buckets and spades. There are nine to spot.

words

These boxes help you find out what tricky words mean.

Photo acknowledgements: **Bigstock**: 7 (Gorilla),
21t (NATASHA17), 22 (Ivonnewierink); **Corbis**: 12 (Underwood
& Underwood), 14 (The Francis Frith Collection); **Discovery
Picture Library**: 5 (Chris Fairclough), 11 (Chris Fairclough),
21c (Chris Fairclough); **Mary Evans Picture Library**:
4, 10b, 16t (Pharcide), 16b (Barry Norman Collection),
20; **Shutterstock**: beachball art (Virinaflora), word box hut
(AnastasiaN), seaside icons (Aleksandra Novakovic), heading
strips (Inna Ogando), cover and title page (Mark William
Richardson), 9 (Sean Locke Photography), 15 (Dmitry Naumov),
17 (Jo Chambers), 19tr (Emma Manners), 19b (David Hughes);
Small Packages: 13; **sprout.uk.com**: bucket and spade
art; **West Sussex County Council**: 8; **Wikimedia**:
6 (Harold FB Wheeler/The Book of Knowledge), 10cr (Lady's
World), 18 (Detroit Publishing/Photoglob Zürich).

CONTENTS

SEASIDE HOLIDAYS

The seaside is a lovely place for a holiday. You can enjoy the fresh air, relax on the beach or have fun in the sea. There are lots of other things to do, too.

Deal - Bandstand and Pier.

Seaside **resorts** became popular about 200 years ago. Sometimes a whole factory or mine shut down for the week so that all its workers and their families could go on holiday – and everyone went together to the same resort!

Let's go to the pier.

resort
A place where people go on holiday.

Today, people choose when and where to go on holiday. Many people just go to the seaside for the day. Families with children go away in the school holidays. Summer is the busiest time, because that is when the weather is warmest.

GETTING THERE

Preparing for a holiday is exciting. Will you be able to fit everything in your suitcase? At last the big day arrives and it's time to travel to your resort.

Long ago, holidaymakers went to a nearby seaside town squashed into open-topped, horse-drawn coaches called **charabancs**. Later, there were motor charabancs that had engines like cars. Trains were best for going longer distances. Until about 70 years ago, they were steam-powered, and very noisy and smoky! Then modern electric trains started running.

All aboard for the seaside!

charabanc
An early type of coach. The first ones were horse-drawn and had no roof!

Today, many people drive their own cars on holiday. Some still take trains or coaches, or they ride bikes or motorbikes. Others take a plane or ferry and stay at a resort in another country.

SOMEWHERE TO STAY

When you go away on holiday, you need a place to stay. There are hotels, B&Bs, apartments, villas, holiday camps and campsites.

Lots of seaside towns have grand old hotels along the seafront. Many were built in the 1800s. The rooms did not usually have their own bathroom, but the ones at the front had beautiful views of the sea!

In the 1950s and 1960s, holiday camps were popular. Families stayed in wooden huts called chalets. There were activities, such as ballroom dancing, entertainments and funny competitions.

Holidaymakers still stay in hotels – but these days they don't usually have to share a bathroom! Other people rent cottages or stay on campsites in tents or caravans.

B&B
A guest house that offers bed and breakfast to paying guests.

SUN

READY FOR THE BEACH

Lots of people like to spend time at the beach. They take everything they might need for the whole day, including chairs, rugs, picnics and clothes.

Long ago, families often wore everyday clothes to the beach – long dresses for the ladies and stiff suits for the men. It was rude to show bare skin. Bathing costumes covered most of the body but people still didn't like to be seen on the beach in them. Instead of walking to the sea in their costumes, they got wheeled down in changing huts called **bathing machines**!

23 SOUTHSEA. — View of Beach from

bathing machine

A changing hut that could be wheeled down into the sea.

In the 1920s, sunbathing became a big craze. Swimsuits showed off more skin so people could get a tan. Nowadays we know about the sun's harmful rays. We wear suncream and hats to protect ourselves, or we sit under a beach umbrella.

FUN ON THE SAND

There are **so many fun things to do** on the beach. Some people enjoy just sitting and watching the waves. Others like being busy.

shrimping net

A long-handled net for catching fish and other creatures from shallow water.

Beach games have not changed much. Families still play tag and catch. Football, cricket, bowls and volleyball are all popular sports. Children still like exploring rock pools with **shrimping nets**, too.

Long ago, just like today, children played in the sand and built sandcastles with moats. They even had buckets and spades – but theirs were made of tin and wood, not plastic.

Not all holidaymakers stay on the beach all day. Walking along cliff paths is exciting – and from that high up, you can see for miles!

FUN IN THE WATER

What makes the seaside different to everywhere else? The sea and its tides! At high tide the water moves up the beach, and at low tide it falls away again.

The wind brings waves that are good for jumping over. It is lovely to paddle, splash and swim in the sea. There are lots of water sports, too. Surfing and windsurfing took off in the last 50 years. People also enjoy bodyboarding, kite surfing and sailing.

DANGER!
The sea has strong currents that can carry you out to sea.

Some children long ago were lucky enough to have small wooden canoes to play in at the seaside. Today there are all sorts of plastic boats and **inflatable** toys for having fun in the sea. Never go too far from shore, though.

inflatable
Something that can be filled up with air so it floats.

SEASIDE RIDES

Rides are a big attraction at seaside resorts. There are animal rides on the beach, exciting funfair rides and special trains and trams for tourists.

Some places still have old **funicular lifts** running. Most were built more than a century ago. They have pairs of carriages that take passengers up and down the cliff.

People enjoyed funfairs long ago, just as they do today. The first rollercoasters were not as fast as modern ones – but passengers made the same gasps and screams.

The Lifts, Folkestone.

Wheee!

funicular lift

A lift made up of pairs of cable cars that travel up and down cliffs.

Many other fairground rides have hardly changed. People still love dodgem cars, ferris wheels and merry-go-rounds.

Animal rides are not as common today, though. Long ago, most beaches in Britain had donkey rides or goat cart rides in the summer months. Today, only a few resorts still have donkeys.

PIER AND PROMENADE

Holidaymakers flocked to the pier and the promenade. There were lots of entertainments on the pier. The promenade was the place to take a stroll.

promenade
The walkway or pavement along the seafront.

Long ago, the promenade was where families showed off their best clothes and breathed the sea air. Today all sorts of people use it, including dog walkers, rollerskaters and joggers.

That's the way to do it!

Many piers were built in the 1800s to attract tourists. They look like a bridge jutting into the sea and have buildings on them. People paid to go on the pier. There were side shows, such as Punch and Judy and fortune-tellers. Most piers had a music hall, a bandstand and an arcade. Today's piers have bars, nightclubs, amusement arcades and funfairs.

POSTCARDS AND SOUVENIRS

In the past, people always sent their friends and family postcards to show where they were on holiday. The postcards had photos of the resort or funny cartoons.

Not many people send postcards today. They can take a picture of themselves on holiday on their smartphone. Then they can post it online with a message to all their friends instead.

Ventnor, looking East

The Sands, Bognor

PORTHMINSTER BEACH & POINT. ST. IVES.

People still buy **souvenirs**, though. Souvenir shops sell mugs, china ornaments and tea towels with pictures of the resort on them. Some sell ornaments or jewellery made of seashells. People also buy sticks of rock, lollipops and tins of fudge or biscuits. These make great presents for relatives or neighbours.

THE SANDS, SKEGNESS

souvenir
Something that helps you remember a place. It can be something you find or something you buy.

THINGS TO DO

Now you've found out lots about seaside holidays today and long ago. Are you ready for a project? Here are some ideas for fantastic follow-on activities:

1. Write a holiday postcard
Draw a seaside scene on a blank postcard. Who will you send it to? On the back, write your message on the left and the person's address on the right. Now pop on a stamp and post it!

2. Carry out a beach survey
In class, or with a group of friends, find out what beach activities people like most. Put the results in a table – write the activities in the first column and how many like them in the second column.

3. Make a sandwich
Create the perfect sandwich for a beach picnic. What filling will you use? Carefully cut the sandwich into four and then pop it in a lunchbox to keep it fresh.

4. Design a flag for a sandcastle
The best sandcastles are topped with a flag! Fold a thin rectangle of plain paper in half and glue it around a drinking straw (the flagpole). Draw your flag design on both sides. Don't forget to take it with you next time you visit the beach – or even a sandpit!

5. Make a game of seaside pairs
Pairs is a great memory game. Cut out 24 small card squares. Choose 12 seaside images – for example, an ice-cream, crab or sandcastle – and copy each onto two cards. To play, turn the cards face down. Take turns to turn over two cards. If you find a matching pair, keep them. The winner is the one with most cards at the end.

NOTES FOR ADULTS

The **Beside the Seaside** series has been carefully planned to provide an extra resource for young children, both at school and at home. It supports and extends their learning by linking to the KS1 curriculum and beyond.

In Geography, a foundation subject at this level, the seaside is a rich and popular topic because it allows children to:

1a Ask geographical questions [for example, 'What is it like to live in this place?']

1c Express their own views about people, places and environments [for example, residents and tourists, resort attractions and places to stay]

2a Use geographical vocabulary [for example, near, far, north, south, coast, cliff]

2d Use secondary sources of information [for example, CD-ROMs, pictures, photographs, stories, information texts, videos, artefacts]

3a Identify and describe what places are like [for example, in terms of landscape, jobs, weather]

3c Recognise how places have become the way they are and how they are changing [for example, the importance of the fishing industry]

3d Recognise how places compare with other places [for example, compare a seaside town to a city]

4a Make observations about where things are located [for example, a bandstand on a pier or in a public park] and about other features in the environment [for example, seasonal changes in weather]

It also provides plenty of opportunities for crossover work with other subjects.

The four titles in this series split the seaside into four sub-topics:
Seaside Holidays Then and Now
Seaside Jobs
Seaside Plants and Animals
Seaside Towns

In addition to Geography, the four books support the core subjects of English, Mathematics and Science and other foundation subjects such as Art and Design, Design and Technology and History – especially if children are encouraged to get involved in the suggested extension activities on the facing page.

Reading with children
When children are learning to read, they become more confident and make quicker progress if they are exposed to as many different types of writing as possible. In particular, their reading should not only focus on fiction and stories, but on non-fiction too. The **Beside the Seaside** books offer young readers different levels of text – for example, straightforward factual sentences and fun speech bubbles. As well as maintaining children's interest, these offer children the opportunity to distinguish between different types of communication.

Make the most of your reading time. Whether it is the adult or the child who is reading, he or she should try to follow the words with his or her fingers – this is useful for non-readers, reluctant readers and confident readers alike. Pausing in your reading gives a chance for questions and to discuss the content of the pictures. For reluctant readers, try turning the reading into a game – perhaps you read alternate pages, or the child only reads speech bubble text. To further encourage interactivity with the content, there is a small artwork of a bucket and spade hidden on every main spread for children to find.

INDEX